CORN SNAKES AND RED RATS

Welcome to the world of the Corn Snake, *Elaphe guttata*, the first truly domesticated reptile. Less than 50 years ago it was difficult to find any detailed and informative material on the natural history of the species, although it is one of the most common and often conspicuous snakes over two-thirds of the United States. Bright reddish orange specimens from Florida and the Carolinas were popular display animals in roadside snake emporiums (few zoos yet had any user-friendly snake displays), and many college biology laboratories kept a few specimens alive in homemade wooden terraria for a few weeks before placing them in the permanent formalin collection for further reference. Collectors occasionally turned up a few nests and recorded the number of eggs present, but most observations were purely incidental to collecting for the specimen jar.

In the late 1950's Corn Snakes arrived on the snake-breeding scene for the first time with the production of many litters of hatchlings in the laboratory. These were bred mostly to study inheritance of albinism and other characters noted in wild-caught individuals, but they were a start

Although the Red Rat Snake, *Elaphe guttata,* is one of the most widespread serpents in the United States, very little was known about it until some 50 years ago. Shown is the questionable "Lower Keys" form, *Elaphe guttata "rosacea."*

PHOTO BY R. D. BARTLETT.

in the right direction. By the mid-1970's Corn Snakes were becoming fairly well-known as living animals in the scientific literature. It was just a matter of time before their many excellent keeping qualities would push them out of the laboratory into the waiting arms of herpetoculturists (reptile and amphibian breeders) looking for that "perfect" animal to promote the budding hobby to the masses.

In 1988 it was estimated that some lines of Corn Snakes had been in captivity for ten or more captive-bred generations. Over the previous two decades Corn Snakes slowly but steadily had become abundant pets available in almost any pet shop, and they were available in color patterns never seen in the wild. The Corn Snake today can be considered a truly domesticated animal, widely bred in captivity from parents that have never seen the wild, produced in breeds not seen in nature, and totally dependent on man for the continuation of its bloodlines.

Is the situation today in the Corn Snake much different from that in the domestic Dog? Everyone knows that the common pet Dog, in all its dozens of carefully standardized breeds, is simply a Wolf, *Canis lupus*, that has been bred to fit the requirements of mankind. In the process the single species has received two different common names, one for the wild ancestor (Wolf) and the other for the manmade domesticated form

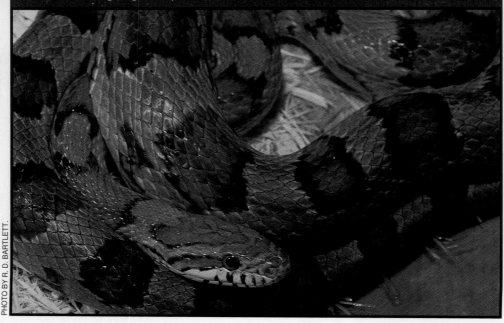

Corn Snakes are considered by many to be one of the first truly domesticated snake species. In fact, in this book I will refer to domestic specimens of *Elaphe guttata* as "Corn Snakes," while giving wild specimens the name "Red Rat Snake."

PHOTO BY R. D. BARTLETT.

PHOTO BY R. D. BARLETT.

The Great Plains Rat Snake, *Elaphe emoryi,* was for many years considered a western subspecies of the Corn Snakes (thus it was known as *E. g. emoryi*), but has since been elevated to full species rank. This attractive animal has never enjoyed the same ground-shaking popularity as its eastern cousin.

(Dog). Left to their own devices, Dogs will revert to Wolves (at least somewhat, though never fully recapturing the majesty of their ancestor). Without man's help, the most spectacular blood Corn or snow Corn, if allowed to breed freely with others of its species, natural or manmade, will revert to something resembling a wild Corn Snake. The major difference in the two situations is that the Dog has been domesticated over at least 3,000 years to exist in at least 200 recognizable breeds, while the Corn Snake has been domesticated for only 30 years and exists in just a few dozen breeds.

I think that the time has come to give the manmade Corns their due. In this book I will be using different common names for "natural" and "manmade" *Elaphe guttata.* **Corn Snake** will be applied to captive-bred breeds and individuals, those that have a lineage distinct from wild snakes. To the wild *Elaphe guttata* I will be applying the common name **Red Rat Snake**, an epithet that has gained wide acceptance in the scientific literature and helps make it obvious that the species is indeed another rat snake of the genus *Elaphe* along with the American Rat Snake (*Elaphe obsoleta*), Baird's Rat Snake (*E. bairdi*), the Fox Snake (*E. vulpina*), and almost three dozen other species spread over the Northern Hemisphere.

Additionally, I'm going to break with the traditional usages for subspecies in the Red Rat Snake, recognizing the western populations as a full species, the **Great Plains Rat Snake,** *Elaphe emoryi.* This usage is gaining ground in the scientific literature and makes some sense, as we'll see in a later chapter devoted just to this species. Though not as colorful as the Red Rat, the Great Plains Rat is an excellent pet and even has provided a few genes used in creating some of the manmade Corn Snake breeds.

If you want more information on the rat snakes in general, I suggest you try my other books on the subject, both published by T.F.H.: *Rat Snakes: A Hobbyist's Guide to* Elaphe *and Kin*, Staszko & Walls, 1994 (TS-144); and *Rat Snakes*, 1994 (RE-110). Both (but especially the former title) will give you a good survey of *Elaphe* and close allies and are fully illustrated in color. After all, once you've bred a few Corn Snakes you probably will want to move on to other, somewhat more difficult rat snakes, many species and subspecies of which are readily available through pet shops.

Of the many "manmade" Corn Snakes varieties, one of the more interesting is the "snow Corn." Most snow Corns have an absence of coloration because both black and red pigments are missing from the pattern, but others, like the stunning specimen shown here, display much yellow pigment.

PHOTO BY R. D. BARTLETT, COURTESY OF RANDI SHERMAN.

RED RAT SNAKES

HISTORY

The Red Rat Snake, *Elaphe guttata*, was named and formally described by Linnaeus in 1766, making it one of the first described North American snakes. It of course was known much earlier and even was figured by early naturalists from specimens taken in the Carolinas. The type locality entire southeastern United States) until it gets to Florida, where several trends in color and scalation appear. This species, by the way, is the type of the genus *Pantherophis* of Fitzinger, 1843, something to remember if (as seems likely) American *Elaphe* eventually are found to differ from

The Red Rat Snake was formally described by Swedish physician and naturalist Carl von Linne (aka Carolus Linnaeus) in 1766, making it one of the first snakes in North America to have a scientific name.

PHOTO BY R. D. BARTLETT.

has been restricted on historical evidence to near Charleston, South Carolina. Early American naturalists had a lot of trouble with this snake, describing it repeatedly under a variety of names that today are all considered synonyms. Remarkably, the species actually shows little variation over its large range (the the Eurasian type-species at the generic level.

The Red Rat Snake has been more commonly called the Corn Snake in most literature, but as mentioned earlier there is a strong trend to calling it the Red Rat Snake in the scientific literature. I've already discussed the restriction here of the common

PHOTO BY R. D. BARTLETT.

The name "Red Rat Snake" is based on the animal's coloration, which is one of its major distinguishing features (although some specimens seem more orange than red).

name Corn Snake to captive-bred breeds. Corn Snake of course refers to the common occurrence of the snake in corn cribs of barns from earliest times to today, the snake living in barns and feeding on mice and rats. Red Rat Snake emphasizes the major distinguishing feature of the species, its coloration, that separates it from the Great Plains Rat Snake.

Obviously derived from *Elaphe emoryi* or a form directly ancestral to the two species, Red Rats probably have been separated from their western relative by the Mississippi River for two million years or less. The current range reflects at least in part the alternating cool, dry glacial periods (when so much water was tied up in icecaps that ocean levels dropped tremendously and produced large areas of new coastline) and warm, wet interglacials or pluvials (as icecaps melted the sea levels rose, drowning out coastal populations except at higher elevations) that have controlled the vegetation and fauna of the eastern United States since then. The most northern populations (as in Maryland and New Jersey) probably have been present in these states for only the few thousand years since the glaciers last retreated, while at least some populations in Florida probably represent primitive relicts trapped on islands formed during wet interglacials when rising sea levels drowned most of the Florida Peninsula. Over most of the range of the species, individuals and local populations are almost as variable as the species as a whole.

It is quite easy to confuse juvenile or dull adult Red Rat Snakes with juveniles and subadults of the American Rat Snake, *Elaphe obsoleta*. The complete spearpoint on top of the head usually works (absent in all *E. obsoleta*), but some Red Rats have the head pattern reduced and the spearpoint broken. In these cases look at the stripe running from the eye to the corner of the mouth; in Red Rats the stripe has black outlines and a reddish brown center and extends beyond the lips onto the throat, while in American Rats the stripe is a solid color and stops at the angle of the jaws.

DESCRIPTION

Red Rats are rather slender snakes with a bread-loaf-shaped body, the ventral scales (the wide ones under the belly) being sharply angled upward near their outer edges as an adaptation for climbing. The scales of the back are weakly keeled on the middle five or so rows, often appearing virtually smooth in juveniles. The scales of the body usually are in 25-27-19 rows (25 about a head length behind the head, 27 at midbody, and 19 in front of the vent). There are almost always 8 supralabials (scales along the upper lip) and 11 infralabials (scales along the lower lip). The ventral scales vary from 205 to 244, males having five or six fewer ventrals than females in any particular population. The number of subcaudals (scales under the tail, of course) varies from 47 to 84 pairs, males having a slightly longer tail than females and thus a few more subcaudals at any locality. There are distinct clines (gradual variation in a character

A very red example of the Red Rat Snake. This specimen was caught in northern Florida.

PHOTO BY R. D. BARTLETT.

Due to the enormous amount of breeding being done with Corn Snakes, there are now a large number of color and pattern varieties available to the interested hobbyist. This striking animal, for example, is known as the "candy cane" Corn Snake. Photo by W. P. Mara.

over a considerable geographic distance) from north to south in the species, specimens from the south generally having more ventrals and subcaudals than those from the northern part of the range. As usual for the genus, the anal scale (the scale covering the vent or cloaca) is divided.

Most Red Rat Snakes live up to their name, being pale reddish orange to brownish orange over the entire back. In the middle of the back is a series of large, usually squarish blotches or saddles about 2 to 5 (or more) scale rows long, each blotch outlined with a black line that may be a full scale wide or reduced to a narrow trace. Typically there are between 25 and 45 saddles present, occasionally 50 in far-southern females. The blotches themselves are some

shade of red-brown to bright red or orange and usually stand in strong contrast to the background color. Often the corners of the blotches extend to meet the corners of the neighboring blotches, especially anteriorly, and may form a broken stripe. Small rounded or elongated (especially anteriorly) reddish spots outlined by black alternate with the main saddles low on the sides, while many specimens show a weak third row of spots where the pattern of the ventral scales joins the lower sides. The first saddle on the neck puts out two arms or broad stripes that extend forward to meet in the center of the head between the eyes, producing the spearpoint characteristic of the species. Additionally, a broad stripe extends from eye to eye over the top of the head and runs back

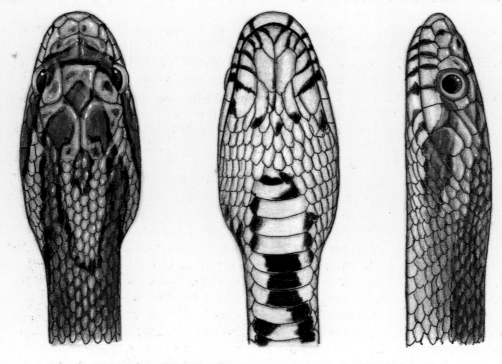

Head study of the Red Rat Snake. Artwork by John R. Quinn.

PHOTO BY R. D. BARTLETT.

This is a hardwood hammock in Florida, home to a population of both Red Rat Snakes and their close relatives the Yellow Rat Snakes, *Elaphe obsoleta quadrivittata*.

from the eye through the angle of the mouth onto the lower throat. The stripe usually is distinctly reddish (often the same shade as the body blotches) and outlined by black. The throat is white and unmarked, the belly also white to pale cream and marked with few to many squarish or rectangular black spots that often reflect bluish. The black pattern of the belly is quite variable individually, some specimens having the belly three-fourths or more black, others with only scattered black spots. Toward the posterior end of the belly the black blotches begin to align at the outer edges of the ventrals and continue past the vent as nearly continuous black stripes on the edges of the tail.

Like the scalation, there are definite trends or clines in the number of blotches (more as you go further south) and their dark outlining (narrower to the south) along the Atlantic Coast, both trends reaching their peak in the southern Florida Keys.

VARIATION

Though the species has been well-studied along the Atlantic Coast, the more interior populations remain poorly studied. As a general rule, northern specimens are rather subdued in color, the dorsal saddles sometimes not very distinct from the background. The broad black outlining of the saddles also increases the dullness of the specimens. From the Carolinas south through most of Florida the colors brighten considerably and contrast increases, leading to highly desirable individuals from many different populations. The bright patterns continue around the

Belly color varies in the other direction, from a stronger tendency to black bellies in the north to a reduced pattern in far-southern Florida. As mentioned, the number of ventrals and subcaudals increases from north to south.

PHOTO BY MICHAEL GILROY.

Red Rat Snakes generally are brightest in coloration in the southern part of their range, although some specimens in peninsular Florida are about as dark as the most northerly ranging specimens. Shown is what would be considered a fairly "bright" specimen.

lower Gulf Coast to eastern Louisiana. Specimens from some western Florida populations are quite dull, however, almost as brown as the western *Elaphe emoryi*, while upland interior specimens (southern Appalachians through Tennessee and Kentucky) may be an undistinguished pinkish gray with mahogany blotches.

Specimens from extreme southern Florida, especially the Lower Keys, are very pale (the "pink phase"), may completely lack black outlines around the saddles, lack most or all the small blotches on the lower sides, and lack all or most of the belly pattern. Such specimens are most typical of the southernmost Keys but also occur on various islands on the southwestern coast of Florida and on the Upper Keys. This "pink phase" long has been known as *E. guttata rosacea* (Cope, 1888) and has been the source of continued disagreement among the various herpetologists who have studied the form. Lower *rosacea* as a distinct subspecies, though the delicately colored "pink phase" specimens continue to be highly desirable specimens for specialist breeders.

Supposed intergradation between *Elaphe guttata* and *E.*

PHOTO BY JOHN IVERSON.

This gorgeous Red Rat Snake, which was secured from the Florida Everglades, is what hobbyists would recognize as a very "bright" specimen.

Keys specimens have always been rare and currently are protected. The most recent published analysis of variation in Red Rat Snakes in Florida determined that the "pink phase" Red Rat is the end of a cline and is not constant in character development, sharing various features with populations from further north in Florida. Thus there seem to be no valid reasons to continue recognition of *emoryi* in Louisiana and adjacent areas is discussed in the chapter on *E. emoryi*.

LENGTH

Red Rats are not large snakes, most being between 2 and 3 feet in length, but with a good number approaching 4 feet. The record stands at 6 feet, but even a 5-footer is virtually unknown today.

RANGE

The basic range of the Red Rat Snake extends from eastern Louisiana (east of the Mississippi River except in the Atchafalaya Basin west of New Orleans) and all of Mississippi (except the Black Dirt region in the northwest) over the southeastern United States to North Carolina. The species is absent from most of Tennessee and known only from two small regions of Kentucky. A large group of populations occurs from central Virginia to New Jersey uninhabitable to these snakes, the northern populations seem to have moved into the area rather recently from an Ice Age refuge isolated for many years, perhaps in Virginia.

NATURAL HISTORY

In modern times the Red Rat Snake has become a snake of developed land, often being found near or in barns and abandoned structures. It also frequents fields and open areas, preferring dry

Certain Red Rat Snakes from the Lower Keys in Florida, those that have greatly reduced black around the saddles and virtually no blotching on the sides and belly, were at one time given their own subspecies classification, *Elaphe guttata rosacea*. These days this taxon is no longer recognized by most herpetologists.

Virginia and southern Maryland across the Delmarva Peninsula into the pinelands of southern New Jersey. It can be safely assumed that the Red Rat Snake was derived from a western ancestor. Because glaciation probably made much of the area from northern habitats to marshland (but not actually being too choosy). Basically, it is a feeder on rodents and nestling birds, and it is found where its prey is most abundant. Juveniles feed on frogs and lizards and even larger insects, but take baby rodents if they can find them.

PHOTO BY R. D. BARTLETT.

In spite of the fact that *Elaphe guttata "rosacea"* is not considered a valid taxon by most herpetologists, Red Rat Snakes carrying the traits of this form are considered desirable by hobbyists because of their stunning beauty.

An active nocturnal constrictor, it unfortunately likes to haunt roads at night, making it easy to collect in numbers in some areas and also easy to die under the wheels of cars. During the day it hides under logs, boards, and other debris or in rodent burrows, and it often has been found in homes. Though it can and does climb well, it usually is terrestrial, perhaps because of competition with the more arboreal American Rat Snake, with which it shares much of its range and habitat.

Depending on locality and the winters in the area, Red Rats are active from March through October or November, though it is possible to find specimens active during mild winters in the southern states. Hibernation (brumation) occurs in the usual types of protected spots such as rotten logs and under structures. Mating occurs shortly after the return of spring activity. For details of mating and egg-laying, see the section on Corn Snake breeding. Natural nests are not commonly found, and until the late 1950's there were few records in the scientific literature. Growth and maturation are rapid, with many or most adults being able to breed when only 18 month to two years old. Full size (or nearly so) may be reached by the age of three or four years.

This can be a long-lived species, with many records in the 18- to 21-year realm and one of 21 years 9 months. Expect average specimens that have adapted to captivity to live at least a dozen years.

Studies of chromosome numbers show 18 pairs of chromosomes (2N=36), the usual number for North American *Elaphe* (as opposed to 2N=40 in *Bogertophis*). The chromosomes can be distinguished only with difficulty from those of the American Rat Snake, *E. obsoleta*.

CAPTIVE CARE AND BREEDING

I'm not going to bother you with a great deal of detail here about keeping and breeding Red Rats in captivity. Instead, I'll go into more detail under these topics for the Corn Snake, by my definition a captive-bred Red Rat. Suffice it to say that Red Rats, if taken while young (18 inches to perhaps 24

Because Red Rats are so conspicuous in the wild, and because they like to roam roadways during the night, they are easy prey for collectors.

PHOTO BY LOUIS PORRAS.

One nice thing about purchasing albino Corn Snakes is that you know you're getting a captive-bred specimen. Wild-caught *guttata* often are loaded with parasites, boast a few scars, and do not adjust to captivity.

the Corn Snakes, of course, and are direct ancestors of the albino, black albino, and blood red breeds in the hobby today. Collectors have long selected oddball patterns from wild-caught specimens for further breeding experiments, leading to many of our modern breeds.

Because of the popularity of the Red Rat Snake among amateur herpetologists, the species has been over-collected throughout it range and continues to be collected in large numbers regardless of local laws in several states restricting or prohibiting collecting for commercial purposes. New Jersey, for instance, outlaws the collecting of all Red Rats in the state and prohibits the keeping of any *Elaphe guttata* in captivity (except, currently, captive-bred albinos). In Florida commercial collecting is restricted and it is theoretically illegal to collect from vehicles (i.e., no road-hunting at night, the easiest way to collect this species). Populations near Baton Rouge, Louisiana, and several spots in the Carolinas have been preyed upon by generations of herpers and have never been common anyway. I personally don't understand why anyone would purchase a Red Rat Snake with all the attendant problems of a wild-caught specimen (aggressiveness, parasite load, scars, often dull and indistinct patterns) when they can purchase nearly perfect Corn Snakes of many types for the same money. Red Rats should be observed in their natural habitat and not kept as pets by amateurs. (Purely personal opinion, mind you.)

inches), are adaptable animals that often feed well on frozen and thawed mice and rat pups. Adults may be nervous, aggressive animals, however, that will have to be force-fed before they learn to take house mice. As long as the terrarium is kept moderately dry, several hide boxes are provided, and there is a more moist area under one of the hides, they will do fairly well. Red Rats (and Corns, for that matter) are notorious escape artists and can get out through the smallest crack in a cover, so beware.

Wild-caught Red Rat Snakes have served as the ancestors to all

There is room in the hobby, however, for some wild-caught Red Rats. Because in-breeding is essential to maintaining the Corn Snake breeds, most breeds are genetically somewhat weakened. This weakness shows as abnormalities among the offspring (especially pug heads, scalation problems, and irregular patterns) and reduced viability of both eggs and young. Only by regular infusions of fresh bloodlines (out-crossing) into captive "populations" can the breeds maintain their strength, and the only available out-cross to the Corn Snakes is the Red Rat Snake. Carefully selected wild-caught specimens could be used to add some life to tired Corn Snake genetic lines, but only in the hands of experienced breeders with large breeding groups of various Corn Snake types. Such out-crossing requires only a few specimens each year to be successful, numbers that selected wild populations certainly could stand.

This might be the best place to mention hybridization between the Red Rat Snake and other species and genera. *Elaphe guttata* has been crossed with a variety of other taxa, including the American Rat Snake (*E. obsoleta*) of various subspecies, the California Kingsnake (*Lampropeltis getula californica*), the Gopher Snake (*Pituophis catenifer*), and supposedly the Milksnake (*Lampropeltis triangulum*) of various subspecies and even the Gray-banded Kingsnake (*Lampropeltis alterna*). According to the breeders, all these crosses produced fertile offspring capable of breeding with others of their

Newborn albino Corn Snakes usually accept pinkie mice, but be careful about housing more than one in the same enclosure—they have been known to eat each other.

Perhaps one of the nicest points about Corn Snakes is that even inexperienced hobbyists can propagate them. The demands in this regard are, after all, quite minimal. In short, you could say that Corn Snakes are excellent "beginner's" snakes for aspiring culturists. Photo by Isabelle Francais, courtesy of Tim M. Scott.

type and their parents. No fancy tricks are required, just a careful substitution of females at the last minute during mating. For a few years these hybrids, some of which are striking and even beautiful animals, were fairly popular though always expensive and hard to obtain, but now they seldom seem to be produced. Perhaps breeders are getting some common sense and asking the question, "What will these hybrids do to breeding programs if they are accidentally introduced into a line?" Because any hybrid-breeding program is sure to produce a multitude of non-exciting specimens much more like the parents than the hoped-for "different" hybrids, the temptation to sell these disappointing snakes as "normals" for the species could be very strong. After all, breeders have to get funds by selling their wares just like any other business. Few breeders keep, or at least make available to customers, accurate pedigrees on their lines, and it is not hard to imagine numbers of hybrids being dumped on the market to be purchased by unsuspecting amateurs and even other breeders. The risks would seem to outweigh the advantages of hybridization.

Hybrid snakes made a slight ripple in the herpetocultural hobby a few years ago, and many of these were the product of something crossed with a Corn Snake. This beautiful specimen, for example, is the progeny of a Corn Snake crossed with a California Kingsnake, *Lampropeltis getula californiae*. Its most-often used common name is the "Jungle Corn."

PHOTO W. P. MARA.

Opacity of the eyes ("blue eye") is a standard trait of snakes that are about to shed. The specimen shown is a melanistic Corn Snake. Photo by Isabelle Francais, courtesy of Tim M. Scott.

BASIC CORN SNAKE CARE

SELECTING A CORN SNAKE

As with any pet, you will only get full enjoyment from a healthy Corn Snake specimen with a good background. Fortunately, selecting your first Corn Snake is easy. You are dealing with a carefully bred, highly selected pure-bred just made to be a pet. Your major problems will be deciding which breed to choose (keeping within your budget) and, especially, deciding if you want to try a hatchling or a yearling Corn. First the age.

Hatchlings typically are made available for sale as soon as they have taken their first pinkie mouse, either live or frozen and then thawed. Corn Snakes, like most other snakes, do not feed immediately upon leaving the egg. They exist for a few days (sometimes as much as a week) on yolk and similar food from the egg retained in the gut. Once they have their first skin shed or molt, they become dependent on outside sources of food. Thus breeders must hold any snake for at least three to ten days until it molts and then takes its first food item.

Breeders have to sell stock to make money, so they cannot afford to hold hatchlings for long before getting them to the market. The number of hatchling Corn Snakes available in pet shops, especially in the autumn, is large, and the prices are relatively cheap for almost any breed.

Hatchlings, however, often have problems that may not appear for several weeks or even months after hatching. 1) Some may not feed well on commercial mice; you don't want to have to force-feed tiny, delicate snakes or, worse yet, have to look for baby lizards or frogs as food for the first six or eight months. 2) Personality varies from snake to snake and will not develop for a few weeks or months. 3) Hatchling Corn Snakes do not necessarily show the real color or even full pattern of the adult. Babies often have much brighter aspects of color in certain patterns (especially those close to wild-types); albinos of various types often have bright orange spots on the back between the saddles; and some breeds such as

PHOTO R. D. BARTLETT, COURTESY OF RANDI SHERMAN.

The head is the first place you will want to check when inspecting a Corn Snake for potential purchase. Look for any signs of ill health such as watery eyes, soft or swollen gums, or runny nostrils. If you're lucky you'll find specimens that suffer from none of these problems, like the beautiful one shown.

blood reds do not develop full, brilliant coloration until mature. 4) There is always the potential for hidden anatomical or behavioral problems in closely in-bred lines that might not show up for months after hatching.

Yearlings (basically snakes from eight months to a year old) should be established feeders on commercial mice and rat pups, they will have developed a nice tame personality if properly handled, and they should by now give you a very good idea of the adult colors and patterns. Additionally, most hidden problems become visible during the first few months of life, and it is unlikely that a tame, good-looking snake that is feeding well will have many problems to develop later in life. However, a yearling may cost four or five times as much as a hatchling of the same breed—they've eaten many mice over the last few months and taken up space and time for the breeder.

For the average amateur, hatchlings probably are too chancy and you would be better off with a yearling. Remember that the average Corn Snake will live 12 or more years, so your initial investment in a good animal is not really too much considering the quality of pet you are getting.

THE TERRARIUM

For starters, be sure that you purchase your terrarium or habitat before you get your snake. Also be sure that you get all the extras and essentials at the same time—heaters, lights, locking lid, substrate, hide boxes. Cardboard boxes and gallon jars are not suitable containers of Corn Snakes even for a few hours.

The usual all-glass aquarium from your local pet shop makes an

Enclosure arrangements for Corn Snakes need not be elaborate. As long as they have clean bedding, fresh water, a place to hide, and something to climb on, they'll do fine.

PHOTO BY ISABELLE FRANCAIS.

For transport or temporary holding of small Corn Snake specimens, plastic shoeboxes are ideal. For larger specimens, you will want to use plastic sweaterboxes. The variety shown is a striped albino.

adequate terrarium for your Corn Snake. It is cheap, easy to find, comes in several sizes, and is designed to fit many different styles of lids and lights. A 20-gallon long (30 X 12 X 12 inches) is suitable for one or two Corn Snakes of all sizes and will give a young snake plenty of room to grow. Corn Snakes are relatively sedentary and secretive and, other than trying to find that weak spot in the lid in order to escape, do not need a large cage in which to exercise. A 20-gallon tank fits well on many table tops and doesn't need a special stand.

Your pet shop may be able to special-order a plastic or wood and formica cage with sliding glass doors for your pet. These handsome cages are relatively expensive but will last for years and can be ganged into nice wall units of various types to accommodate many sizes of Corns.

Any terrarium must have a complete lid, preferably of fine screen or glass and screen, that locks securely at all corners. Don't try to get by with just a brick or something else heavy on top; it won't work. Corns are excellent climbers, and babies can even climb up the silicone cement holding the glass together at the corners. The lid also provides a barrier between the snake and the lights and helps prevent burns.

LIGHTS

Corn Snakes are nocturnal and don't really need special lighting. However, it won't hurt to have a full-spectrum fluorescent bulb over the tank to provide a bit of ultraviolet. The light can be used to provide a day length of about 12 hours in midsummer,

PHOTO COURTESY OF ISABELLE FRANCAIS, COURTESY OF BILL AND MARCIA BRANT.

Corn Snakes, like most other snakes, are curious creatures that will not think twice before slithering out of their enclosure to roam around. Make sure you have all cages well secured!

Providing your Corn Snakes with correct photoperiod (day/night cycle) is very important. Bulbs designed specifically for the keeping of reptiles and amphibians now are available at many pet shops, and some provide not only light but a measure of heat as well.

PHOTO COURTESY OF CORALIFE/ENERGY SAVERS.

decreasing to eight hours or less the rest of the year. Check your pet shop for a correct reptile light.

You also need a basking light, usually an incandescent bulb in a reflector holder. Position this so it shines onto a flat rock or similar decoration to provide a warm basking spot for at least four or five hours a day and then can be turned off when the snake becomes active at night. The rock will remain warm for several hours. Such a basking light is a supplement to the undertank heater we'll discuss shortly.

HEATING

Corn Snakes do well at air temperatures between 75 and 80°F (24 and 27°C) during the day, dropping by five to ten

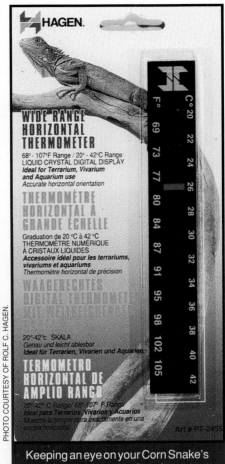

Keeping an eye on your Corn Snake's terrarium temperature is an important facet of good husbandry. If the animal is allowed to become too warm or too cold, it could become ill. Fortunately, high-range thermometers designed specifically for herp keeping now are available.

sufficient heat to keep a terrarium at about 75 to 80°F without other heat sources if the room temperature is kept at a normal level. Used in conjunction with a basking light, this should be all you need to keep your Corn Snake warm and healthy when it is not hibernating.

SUBSTRATES, WATER BOWLS, AND HIDE BOXES

The most simple substrate for the Corn Snake terrarium is a few sheets of white, absorbent paper toweling from the kitchen. This is sanitary, easy to replace, and cheap. A snake doesn't know the difference between substrates as long as it works to keep it dry and clean. Owners, however, like a

Be sure to place your Corn Snakes in a safe place when cleaning their enclosures. A plastic garbage can (with a lid, of course) is acceptable for this purpose.

degrees at night. Use a thermometer (the plastic strip types are fine) in the terrarium to be sure of the temperature—do not guess.

Without doubt the best type of heater today is the undertank heating pad designed specifically for reptile terraria. Many types are available at your pet shop. When placed correctly they provide

Undertank heating pads work well with Corn Snakes. A keeper can warm only one particular section of the enclosure, giving the inmate more than one temperature zone to choose from.

Wood shaving (also known as excelsior) make a good bedding for a Corn Snake's enclosure. Wood shavings are easy to work with, absorbent, and fairly inexpensive. The specimen shown is a "reverse Okeetee" albino.

If you are looking for substrate that is easy to work with and not terribly naturalistic in appearance, a terrarium liner will do nicely. Many pet shops now carry these in different sizes to fit different sizes of enclosure.

the rest of the terrarium so the Corn Snake can more adequately satisfy its moisture requirements.

Corn Snakes drink, so provide a small, stable water bowl and fill it with clean water each day. For some reason Corns don't tend to curl up and soak in their water bowls too often, and most seldom defecate in the water, which makes them easier to keep clean than many other pet snakes.

They do need hide boxes, however, preferably at least two in any terrarium. As mentioned, keep one a bit more moist than the other. Position one near the heater and the other in the coolest corner of the tank so the snake can have a heat gradient and become comfortable at the temperature it needs at any time of the day or night. Many attractive hides are available at your pet shop, but

fancier substrate that looks more natural even though it causes more complications and is more expensive than paper.

Corn Snakes will accept any of the standard substrates, from fine, smooth sand (disliked by some keepers because it supposedly could cause gut impactions and shedding problems) to peat moss and wood shavings (never cedar, which is reported to be toxic). You want a material that will not become too wet, because Corn Snakes like tanks on the drier side. The area under one of the hide boxes should be kept more moist than

Organic substrates like crushed bark work well with Corn Snakes. Most are easy to work with, pleasing to the eye, and can be bought in bulk quantities.

beware those that are too complicated to keep clean easily. Also, do not try to be "kind" to the Corn Snake and give it a roomy hide box. Snakes like to relax with their sides and back touching a surface, so they prefer to rest in tight quarters.

As for decorations, a sturdy, low climbing branch (one that can be cleaned regularly and does not have bark that could harbor mites) will be used if provided. Be sure it does not come too close to the lid or the Corn might be able to use the height to its advantage to help lift the lid. Corn Snakes are constrictors and incredibly strong for their small size. Plants are a waste in the Corn Snake terrarium, although you can provide attractive plastic plants if you want them—the snake will not care at all. The more simply the terrarium is furnished, the easier it will be to keep clean.

FEEDING

Although the Red Rat Snake feeds on a variety of prey animals, ranging from frogs and lizards (and even insects) when young to

Every captive Corn Snake needs a waterbowl, and that bowl should be cleaned out and fresh water added at least once every two days (every day is preferable).

PHOTO BY ISABELLE FRANCAIS.

Since Corn Snakes like to climb around in their terrarium, like this beautiful striped albino is doing, do yourself a favor and give them a waterbowl that is either very heavy or wider at the base than the mouth. This way the bowl won't tip and you won't be cleaning up the dampened substrate every day.

rodents, bats, and birds when adults, your Corn Snake does not need much variety at all. Remember that this snake is equivalent to a household Dog. Its can of dog food is the commercial mice and rat pups readily available from your pet shop. Mice come in various sizes, from pinkies (only a day or two old, sightless, and hairless), through fuzzies (mobile but not yet weaned, and with a coat of fine hair) to weanlings and adults. Rat pups are hairless or nearly so and about the size of an adult mouse.

The frequency and number of mice fed should vary with the size and activity of the snake, of course. Hatchlings should take a pinkie every two days; if they remain hungry, give them two. You'll seldom overfeed a Corn Snake unless you literally stuff it. As the snake grows older, increase the size of the mouse given and also increase the number of days

between feedings. Adult Corn Snakes do well, in most cases, on one feeding a week of rat pups, the number suited to the size and appetite of the snake.

Many owners agonize over the decision of whether to feed living mice to their Corn Snake. There is little doubt that most snakes do prefer living food over frozen and thawed items, but any good Corn Snake specimen should be adaptable to frozen foods. Corns do not really need exercise such as chasing mice around a terrarium; most are very sedentary animals anyway. Mice (other than pinkies and probably fuzzies) could inflict injuries on Corns— they will defend themselves and have good teeth. Even a small mouse bite to the head could result in an unsightly scar, though the snake is not really bothered by it. The old bit of

There are a number of specialty products available in pet shops that allow you to gain a better grasp on the more subtle aspects of snake keeping.

PHOTO COURTESY OF CORALIFE/ENERGY SAVERS.

advice about never leaving a living rodent in a snake cage overnight is true; snakes have been killed by innocuous-looking mice.

Additionally, humane treatment of mice and rats means that they should not suffer when being used as food. If you decide to leave a mouse in the terrarium for a few hours, give it a pellet of food to chew on. Mice are not very smart and their nature is such that they tend to rapidly ignore predators that are not actively chasing them at the moment. Some areas have laws prohibiting the feeding of living rodents to snakes in public and even have very specific rules about how the mice must be presented.

Thawed rodents provide none of these problems, though they are a bit more difficult to feed. They must be **completely** thawed, including the gut, before being fed. Microwaving will dry out the legs and make the mouse unsavory to the snake, but if the mouse is just left out to thaw for a few hours it could become a bacterial slag heap and dangerous to the snake as well. Try thawing a frozen mouse in a glass of warm water, which should provide a uniform body temperature and hydrated limbs as well. Practice will make perfect.

It probably won't hurt to provide occasional supplements of reptile vitamins and calcium, especially for hatchlings and young snakes. Mice should provide a complete and balanced diet for your Corn Snake, unless the mice were raised on inferior foods themselves. Since there is no way to easily check the nutritional value, a few vitamins

Many snake keepers prefer to give their Corn Snakes pre-killed rather than live mice, mainly because they do not want the food animal to harm the snakes.

PHOTO BY ISABELLE FRANCAIS, COURTESY OF TIM M. SCOTT.

Corn Snakes rarely have trouble securing their meals. Nevertheless, it is advisable that a keeper observes all feeding involving live food items.

and minerals every week or two should provide a safety factor just in case. The thawed mouse can be rolled in a bit of the powder or, if you have access to a syringe, a liquid supplement can be injected into the body cavity.

As a last note, remember that Corn Snakes are nocturnal animals and used to feeding at night. At first, present the food after the lights go down, putting the bodies in a constant spot that the snake can learn to associate with food. Most Corn Snakes rapidly become ravenous feeders that will take any food as soon as it is presented, and some even learn to feed from the keeper's hand with time. A tame, beautiful Corn Snake feeding from your hand is about the ultimate that you can expect from any snake pet.

MITES

Though snakes may be afflicted with many diseases and parasites, your captive-bred Corn Snake should be less susceptible to these than would wild-caught snakes. It always is best, however, to take your snake to a competent veterinarian specializing in reptiles for a complete checkup after you have purchased it. The vet will check the snake for worms of various types and treat them if necessary. An inspection for mites also will be made.

Mites are the only serious parasites likely to be on your Corn Snake, and they are easily treated. The size of small dark pinpoints, they feed on the blood of the snake, usually hiding in the decorations during the day and feeding at night. You can easily control the mites on both the snake and its cage.

ISABELLE FRANCAIS, COURTESY OF BILL AND MARCIA BRANT.

Due to their aggressiveness and occasional viciousness with live foods, Corn Snakes may be a little too graphic in their eating habits to be displayed to the casual observer.

To kill mites on the snake, first try the cheap and effective method of drowning them. Put the snake in a bath of warm (not hot) water for 30 minutes, using a screen to hold it under the surface so only the snout projects into the air (so the snake can breathe, of course). This leaves mites on the head, but these are few in number and can be wiped off to some extent. Alternatively, the snake can be sprayed (not on the head) with a pyrethroid (synthetic pyrethrin) spray available from your veterinarian or a specialized pet shop. The snake is sprayed and then immediately wiped down. The spray also is used on the cage and all decorations that cannot be thrown away or sterilized by heat or chlorine bleach (of course the snake cannot be present at the time); remember to wipe everything off before returning the snake to the terrarium.

Hatchling Corns may be greatly stressed by mites and also by mite treatments. It is best to keep the terrarium as clean as possible and be on a constant lookout for mites before they multiply to problem numbers. Old treatments such as the use of desiccants (silica gel) and dichlorvos insecticide strips today are considered very dangerous to the animals.

Remember that if you have a problem with your Corn Snake, your vet could be its best friend and savior.

BREEDING CORN SNAKES

If you are keeping a Corn Snake as a pet, you probably have in the back of your mind the possibility of eventually getting a pair and breeding them. First, be aware that you will not make any money breeding Corn Snakes, or probably any other species for that matter. Corn varieties obtain a high price in the market only when they are new and restricted in availability. By the time you bought yours in a pet shop, hundreds—perhaps thousands—of that color breed had been produced and sold at ever-declining prices for the breeders. Developing new color breeds may require several generations of experimental breeding, with many failures and almost worthless "mongrels" being produced before the breakthrough, if the breakthrough ever comes. Second, each generation of Corn Snakes takes at least two years to mature to produce viable eggs and young. During this time each snake may eat 80 to 150 mice of various sizes, assuming you started with an inexpensive hatchling. Mice are not cheap unless you breed them yourself, and that's an entirely different chore than going by the pet shop each week or month.

If you decide to breed Corn Snakes, do so because you enjoy the thrill of bringing new life into the world and continuing a line that has been carefully bred for years. If you want to do elaborate breeding programs, the record-keeping alone will drive you crazy and you will have to consider ways of managing several dozen young Corns at one time while waiting for them to mature. I obviously don't have room to go into such detail here, so I'm just going to give you the basics for a simple breeding. Some breeders feel that Corn Snakes are very consistent in their pre- and post-breeding behaviors, including exact timing of skin shedding, number of days the female refuses to eat before laying, etc., but few breeders agree on exactly *what* their snakes do *when*. Snakes are individuals like all other higher animals, something to keep in mind when trying to breed your pet.

SEXING

First, you obviously need a male and a female. Hatchling and young Corn Snakes are very difficult to correctly sex, but by the time your pet is 18 to 24 months old (sexually mature if fed correctly and properly maintained) you should have no trouble sexing it. Males have longer, more slender tails that taper gradually from a wide base, while females have shorter tails that taper more abruptly from a relatively narrower base. This is because the male copulatory organ, the penis, is a complicated structure in snakes. It is deeply split to the base to form what seem to be two separate organs, the hemipenes. The hemipenes

PHOTO BY JEFF GEE.

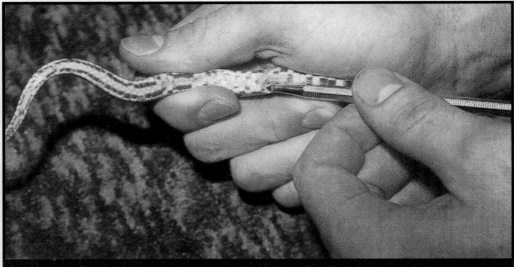

Probing a Corn Snake to determine sex can be a very delicate affair, and an inexperienced person can easily injury the animal in the process.

are hollow sacs covered with various spines and papillae and bearing a groove along one side. The sperm flows along this groove during mating, entering the female's cloaca and then the oviducts. The hemipenes retract into pouches at the base of the tail when not in use. It is the presence of these pouches that makes the base of the male's tail wide and parallel in shape compared to that of the female.

In females there are small scent glands just behind the vent in the same position as the hemipene pouches. These scent glands produce musk, a rather thick, granular material that the female smears along her path when in breeding condition, the scent (along with other scents produced from various glands on the back and the belly) attracting males who are able to identify their own species by the smell.

By using special metal probes (available at most pet shops that deal heavily in snakes), an experienced hobbyist can determine whether any half-grown or adult Corn Snake is a male or a female. The trick is the depth the probe extends when inserted into the opening of the pouch behind the vent. The process can be dangerous if the probe is inserted too far or too energetically, so you should have an expert do the probing and learn the technique by observing it being done. In females the probe will extend the length of only one or two subcaudal scales, while in males it will extend six or eight rows, possibly more.

Thus, you can sex your snake or snakes by the shape of the tail (but you have to see known specimens of the sexes together a few times to see the distinctions) and back it up by probing. You then can purchase a Corn of the opposite sex or perhaps borrow one from a friend to complete the mating. If you have a young male, try to get a large female because successful breeding is more likely with larger females. Males usually are a bit smaller than the females anyway.

BRUMATION

Corn Snakes still respond to natural cycles of temperature and day length, and they must go through these cycles in order for the sperm and eggs to mature sufficiently. Actually, lines that have been in captivity for many generations seem able to successfully breed now regardless of whether or not they have a winter cooling period, but it is best to at least go through the motions to ensure the highest chances of success.

In nature the Red Rat Snake becomes inactive (in most areas) by November, holing up in a rotten stump or some type of cave or crevice until warm weather returns in the spring. Though inactive, they can rapidly respond to warm spells to emerge and sun themselves for a few days until the next cold spell. This type of hibernation is technically called brumation, but most people still call it hibernation. What you have to do with your Corn Snake is to imitate this cooling period for

Breeding an albino Corn Snake to a normally colored Corn should give a litter that looks something like the one shown here. Even the "normal" babies will carry genes heterozygous for albinism.

PHOTO BY K. T. NEMURAS.

about three months and then bring the snake back to normal temperatures. Try to time the cooling period for December through February.

In November gradually reduce the temperature in the terrarium by about 10 degrees over a period of two or three weeks. You are shooting for about 65°F. Reduce the light during the same time and withhold food as well. You want your snake to become inactive and have an empty gut. Provide a water bowl just in case the snake becomes active on exceptionally warm days. The terrarium should not be allowed to become warmer than 70°F, however, until February.

In February gradually let the temperature climb back to normal over a couple of weeks and let the snake bathe and drink freely in order to help free the kidneys from wastes that may have accumulated during brumation. By the time the temperature is back to 75 or 80°F, the snake should be ready to take food again on a regular basis. Mating activity should start shortly after the first post-brumation skin sheds.

MATING

Mating in snakes is very stereotyped, with most species going through basically the same

Very young Corn Snakes don't really need to be hibernated since they won't be ready to breed until they are at least 18 to 24 months old anyway. Shown is a litter of anerythristic or "black albino" specimens.

PHOTO BY K. T. NEMURAS.

Captive-breeding snakes has become something of a sub-industry within the pet business. Some people breed on such a large scale that they need to devote entire rooms to the housing of their stock or, in the example shown here, the many containers used to incubate eggs. Photo by Isabelle Francais, courtesy of Bill and Marcia Brant.

actions, though often differing in details. Basically, the male chases the female, rubbing against her back with his chin (many snakes have scent and sensory glands on the nape and chin) and sides. In nature males have to actively hunt for females, so it perhaps is best to introduce the male into the female's terrarium if they are being kept separately. In the Corn Snake the male does not bite the female on either the head or the back, apparently having lost this behavior found in more primitive species of the genus such as the Fox Snake, *Elaphe vulpina*. Mating is very subdued in Corn Snakes, with just a bit of male coiling about the female before (if ready to mate) she appears to submit.

The male coils his tail about hers and lifts her vent just a bit. She then briefly pops her vent open and the male inserts a hemipenis into the vent. The spines of the hemipenis help hold the organ in position while sperm is transferred into the female. The snakes remain attached for at least 15 minutes, more often 30 minutes (and occasionally several hours), before they separate.

Corn Snakes may mate several times over a few weeks and do not remain paired if other matable individuals are in the terrarium. Thus it is possible to use one good male to breed with several different females or mate an exceptional female with several different males to try to ensure large litters.

The eggs of Corn Snakes are small, immaculate white in color, and vary in number (per clutch) from four or five to up to 30. The best substrates to use for egg incubation are moistened vermiculite and moistened sphagnum moss.

PHOTO BY ISABELLE FRANCAIS.

PHOTO BY R. T. ZAPPALORTI.

The moment of truth for any Corn Snake breeder is when the neonates' tiny heads push through of the shell slits. Average incubation time for Corn Snake eggs is between 50 and 60 days.

LAYING

About 60 days after mating, usually late April or early May, the female will lay her clutch of eggs. Most females stop eating two or three weeks before laying, and usually a female will shed a week or two before the laying begins, signs that it is time to provide her terrarium with a moistened area under her hide box. Many breeders like to provide a dark box of damp, not wet, peat moss for the female. Corn Snakes like to nest in darkness, and many females seem to be fond of laying under a preferred hide box if the substrate under it is moist enough. Do what you must to ensure that a moist, diggable nesting area is available for the pregnant female, otherwise she may not lay and will become eggbound (requiring a trip to the veterinarian and possibly losing the snake) or will deposit her eggs randomly in the cage, where they will dehydrate and die.

Clutches in Corn Snakes vary tremendously, from only four or five eggs in small females to 30 or more in larger females. Obviously larger individuals have more body cavity room to hold more eggs. Corn Snake eggs vary greatly in shape from elongated to almost round and also vary in size. Most females produce elongated eggs about 1.5 inches long, but the shape of the package has little to do with the viability of the embryos within. Females may lay different sizes and shapes of eggs in different clutches. It should be noted that some females lay a second, smaller egg clutch later in the season (females can store sperm for several mating seasons), but this should not be counted upon.

After the female lays, she usually will go about another week or ten days before shedding and then resuming normal feeding behavior. Treat her well while she recovers her energy and food reserves. Start her out with small prey items that take little energy to digest, and reserve the large meals for a month or two after she has begun to eat regularly and returns to her charming old self.

EGGS AND YOUNG

The eggs should be removed (intact if stuck together and always left with the same surface facing up) to an incubator as soon as possible after the female has finished laying. This helps prevent accidents such as being crushed by the parents and dehydration because humidity levels could not be controlled. Incubators can be complicated commercial models or simple plastic boxes filled with damp paper towels or

After the neonates cut through their shells they may still remain in their eggs for a little while. This is normal behavior, and a keeper should not do anything to coax the little snakes out.

PHOTO BY K. T. NEMURAS.

vermiculite. The object is to keep the eggs at a constant temperature of about 80°F (27°C) and close to 100 percent humidity without excessive condensation. (If you let the temperature fluctuate, make sure it drops more often than it rises; temperatures over 85°F can be dangerous, while temperatures down to 75°F just slow development.) An entire book could be written on incubating snake eggs, but perhaps the best procedure is to read several books or articles to get an idea of the various incubation plans used by breeders and hobbyists and then talk to a few keepers who have successfully incubated Corn Snake eggs. Snake egg incubation is far from a science and definitely more of an acquired skill.

Because Corn Snakes lay adhesive eggs, you should remove the entire clump and not try to clean them too much. If you pull the eggs apart you will tear the shells. Put the eggs on the surface of the vermiculite (the material of choice for incubators); do not bury them completely in the substrate. The vermiculite should be kept moist, using a ratio of about one part of water to ten parts of vermiculite. If the eggs begin to collapse, increase the water a bit, but never make the vermiculite wet. The eggs must be able to breathe, and embryos can drown just as readily as they can dehydrate.

At the preferred temperature, hatching should start about 50 to 60 days after laying. Remember that many factors affect development time and there are no exact rules. Incubation times to over 100 days at lower temperatures have been recorded, though often only a few of the eggs ever hatch under such conditions. Try to keep temperatures and humidity constant and you will have a much more predictable hatch.

The young do not all emerge at the same time, so do not be too quick to throw away an egg that has not completely collapsed or exploded. Usually, though, you should be able to see small slits in most of the eggs at about the same time. These are produced by an egg tooth on the snout of the hatchling that is used to cut the way out of the shell. By the time the young slit the shell, their lungs should be developed and they need to breathe air. Weak young that cannot leave the egg within a day or so of slitting may suffocate, and it probably does little harm to give them a hand by further slitting the egg *carefully* with fine scissors or actually cutting a small section out of the egg shell. Carefully slitting eggs that have not yet hatched several days after the rest of the clutch has emerged may save a few very weak or slow young that cannot penetrate the egg shell.

Corn Snake hatchlings vary quite a bit in length, from about 10 inches to 14 inches. Their first shed will occur anywhere from three to seven days after hatching; they then should start feeding on pinkies. The first meal may be a problem. Some hatchlings will take only live pinkies at first, while others may eat only short bloody segments of mouse tails. "Braining" sometimes helps difficult feeders start eating. This rather gruesome process consists of cutting off or opening the top of a pinkie's head and exposing the brain. The scent of blood and brains seems to initiate feeding responses in many hatchlings. Some Corn Snake hatchlings will feed only on small lizards or lizard tails; such young, and those that require force-feeding, probably are beyond the help of beginning Corn Snake breeders.

If kept healthy and fed well, Corn Snakes typically reach maturity at an age of 18 to 24 months and certainly by the age of three years. Most of their growth in length stops by the age of three or four, though growth continues very slowly throughout life as in most snakes. Keeping careful records of your new snakes from hatching throughout life will make keeping and breeding other Corns easier. You can recognize individual Corn Snakes by details of the pattern, but expect these to change somewhat as the snake matures. The colors also can be expected to change somewhat—significantly in some breeds—with time. You won't get rich breeding Corns, but you can expect to have fun and a great learning experience.

Close-up of an albino Corn Snake only moments after cutting through its shell. If you look closely you can see the egg tooth just below the tip of the snout.

DOMESTIC BREEDS

Corn Snakes have gained a great deal of their popularity because of the ready availability of different colors and patterns of captive-bred specimens. It is the very abundance of such variations that gives the Corn Snake its uniqueness in the herpetocultural hobby and the basis for my contention that this is now a domesticated animal.

Because of space considerations I cannot cover every breed here. Additionally, there has been little standardization of breed names as yet, and it is not uncommon for breeders to come up with very different names for animals from the same genetic lines. (New names often sell better than old names, a fact to remember whether you are buying automobiles, videotapes, or Corn Snakes.) Any wholesale listing is likely to have one or two names that appear new, but it often is impossible to determine whether the snakes covered by the names actually are different from other breeds. Also, few breeders keep detailed records of their breeding experiments or actually understand the genetics of the various breeds (which, admittedly, also are largely not understood by scientists). Once a new color or pattern becomes established in Corn Snakes, breeders often are able to cross the new variant with one or more of the established variants, so you can end up with entire series of different breeds becoming available.

In pet shops the most likely color breeds of the Corn Snake to be seen are albinos, anerythristics, and perhaps blood reds, while the pattern breed striped also often is available. Also sold are captive-bred normally patterned animals of especially attractive colors, including a large group of unrelated Corns often called Okeetee Corns. We'll restrict our discussion of Corn Snake breeds mostly to these common types.

COLOR BREEDS

First, a few definitions. An *albino*, amelanistic, or albinistic snake is one that lacks melanin, the dark brown (we usually call it black) pigment that countershades most aspects of the Corn Snake pattern, including especially the edges of the dorsal saddles and the squares on the belly. Albinism is a very complex subject with many different types known, and unfortunately different types of albinos cannot be distinguished externally—you have to do breeding experiments and occasionally chemical tests to distinguish superficially identical types. Melanin is produced in special cells, melanophores, both in the superficial skin layer and deeper in the basal skin strata. The absence of melanin allows the other Corn Snake pigments, especially erythrin (red) and xanthin (yellow) to show through at increased intensities. All this results in the simple fact that no

two albinos are exactly alike even if they come from the same clutch of eggs. Albinos have pink eyes with red pupils.

The pigment *melanin* is produced in the melanophores by changing the chemical structure of an amino acid, tyrosine, with the aid of an enzyme, tyrosinase. Any genetic change that prevents this chemical reaction will produce an albino, and it is known that the genetic change or *mutation* occurs in different chromosome positions in at least two different types of albino Corn Snakes. It thus is possible to cross two similar albinos and produce only *wild-type* (normally patterned) offspring. Further complicating an already complicated story is the fact that albinism is not an all-or-none

Albino Corn Snakes are perhaps the most commonly bred albino snakes in the world. There literally are thousands of these sold in pet shops every year.

Corn Snakes selectively bred for reduced dark pigment often are referred to as "motley Corns." Shown is a two-month old specimen.

situation: the chemical change to produce melanin may be merely weakened or even restricted to just some of the melanophores. In the American Rat Snake, *Elaphe obsoleta*, for instance, a bright tan albino is known. By definition, any snake that lacks melanin is an albino—an albino does *not* have to be all white, and in fact almost no albinos really are white

Corns are albinos that have been selected for exceptionally bright red and orange colors.

Anerythristic (so-called "black albinos") Corn Snakes are the result of a mutation that prevents or greatly reduces the production of erythrin, the red pigment that is so typical of the Corn Snake. Black albinos have a normal pattern, but the only conspicuous

PHOTO BY JIM MERLI.

The striped variety of the Corn Snake, which has been bred in both normally colored and albino forms, is particularly attractive. For some reason, however, they have not become as popular with hobbyists as the standard blotched specimens.

because the red and yellow pigments still are present to outline the normal pattern of the snake.

Snow Corns are virtually white because they have been crossed with anerythristic Corns (see below) and thus lack not only melanin but erythrin, while candy

pigment is melanin. Large adults may be black and gray or tan with a fully developed pattern, with touches of yellow especially on the head and sides. The yellow is from the pigment xanthin, which is not affected by either albinistic or anerythristic mutations. A bright black, tan, and yellow Corn still is

Head of the beautiful and popular "creamsicle" Corn Snake. The breeding formula for this variety is a normal Great Plains Rat Snake crossed with an albino Corn Snake. Photo by Isabelle Francais, courtesy of Tim M. Scott.

a black albino breed.

Both albinos and anerythristics are termed recessive mutations. This means that they only can be seen if the gene for normal coloration is not present in the chromosomes of the snake; normal color masks recessives. A touch of simple genetics is mentioned under the discussion of "creamsicle" Corn production in the Great Plains Rat Snake chapter. I won't go into genetics gene for albinism. Mating the offspring with each other will (theoretically) produce 25% albinos, while mating an offspring back to the albino parent will produce 50% albinos. Snakes that carry a gene for albinism but are not visibly albinos are termed *heteros* or heterozygous for albinism. The same basic rules apply to all recessive mutations in Corn Snakes, as far as known.

Partial albinos or

PHOTO BY ISABELLE FRANCAIS, COURTESY OF TIM M. SCOTT.

If you breed an albino Corn Snake to a "normal," you will get all normally colored offspring. These offspring, however, will possess the albino gene, enabling them to produce albinos later on.

here because most of you wouldn't read it even if I wrote it. Suffice it to say that if you breed two albinos of the same type, you get only albino offspring. If you mate an albino with a wild-type, all the offspring appear normal, but genetically they all carry a *hypomelanistics* are genetically much like true albinos and may actually be just another expression of the same mutation. They have a deficiency of melanin in their skin but still show ghostly traces of the black pattern in the form of a pale tan color. So far this mutation, which has been selected to produce what are called ghost Corns, has not proved especially popular because it simply is not very attractive.

Creamsicles are unusual albinos in that they are hybrids between albinistic Corn Snakes and normal Great Plains Rat Snakes. Their creation is discussed under the latter parent.

Blood red Corns are a different mutation, one in which the erythrin increases in intensity as the snake grows. It might be termed hypererythristic. Because it lacks melanin or has that pigment greatly reduced (including absence of a black belly pattern), the red stands out. Young blood red Corns appear pale reddish with a distinct pattern, but as they grow the pattern becomes overwhelmed with red. Large, selectively bred

"Anerythristic" Corn Snakes are those that have lost their red coloration due to a loss of the pigment *erythrin*. Such snakes are also referred to as "black albinos."

blood red Corn Snakes may appear to be entirely red above and below, making them one of the most striking Corn Snake mutations generally available. Unfortunately, this breed is highly in-bred and there are many reports of reproductive failure, slow growth, and abnormalities in these snakes.

PATTERN BREEDS

Striping is the most common pattern mutation in Corn Snakes. There is a natural tendency in the Red Rat Snake for the small blotches low on the sides and also the corners of the large saddles to extend a bit and even connect into short broken stripes, especially anteriorly. Striping appears to be a common mutation in many snakes with spots on the back, and it usually is recessive to normal patterns. When striped mutations occur in wild snakes the stripes usually are very irregular and may fuse across the back as well as along the length of the body. True striped Corn Snakes possess only dark stripes on the body, with few or no traces of dorsal spotting. An English breeder was able to take an exceptionally well-developed striped Corn Snake and through selective breeding accentuate the stripes. This striped breed can be crossed into albinistic and colorful normal lines to produce truly exceptional snakes. Unfortunately, no two striped Corns are quite alike and the breed has been weakened by in-breeding. Zig-zag Corns are similar to striped Corns but

PHOTO BY ISABELLE FRANCAIS, COURTESY OF BILL AND MARCIA BRANT.

Although some anerythristic Corn Snakes are very attractive, they have never attained the same level of popularity as Corns of the many albino varieties.

connect the blotches and saddles in an irregular fashion rather than regular stripes. This variant also can be bred into various other color lines.

Motley Corns are an unusual breed that has the pattern of the back greatly subdued but present and often partially connected; additionally, it virtually lacks the dark belly pattern. The breed does not appear to be standardized, because many very different-looking Corn Snakes are sold under this name.

NORMAL COLOR BREEDS

Several lines of normally patterned wild-type Corn Snakes are bred and selected for the brightest and most interesting individuals. *Okeetee* Corns originally were derived from very nicely colored (especially deep orange) snakes taken on the property of the Okeetee Club in Jasper County, South Carolina, a

locality once famous for the abundance of its Corn Snakes. Today, unfortunately, the name may be applied to almost anything a breeder wants to sell with a nice name, including some truly dull specimens. Miami Corns are another selectively bred type in which the reddish dorsal saddles stand in strong contrast to a grayish background color. Rosy or pink phase Corn Snakes are those bred to resemble the Lower Keys variant of the Red Rat Snake, with reduced belly pattern, virtual absence of black lines around the dorsal saddles, and an overall pale pinkish red appearance.

Leucistic is an unusual mutation that, though originally rare, has been selectively bred into the American Rat Snake, *Elaphe obsoleta*, and might eventually appear in the Corn Snake through hybridization. (The two species can be made to

Red Rat Snakes generally don't grow over 4 feet in length, making it an easy snake to house in captivity. Another notable captive consideration is the fact that Red Rats like to climb, so a keeper needs to give them plenty of branches. Photo by B. Kahl.

PHOTO BY R. D. BARTLETT.

"Ghost Corns" are hypomelanistic snakes (or *partial albinos*), meaning they have a deficiency of melanin but still retain a "ghostly" trace of it. Ghost Corns never have been terribly popular with hobbyists.

hybridize in the laboratory.) Leucistic snakes are not albinos; instead, they lack the ability to produce *any* pigments in the skin. There thus never are traces of original pattern or areas of color "showing through" the whiteness of the body. Leucistics appear alabaster white in color (due to the iridiophores, cells with reflective platelets), often with black or tan eyes. Unfortunately the mutation that produces the leucistic pattern in the American Rat Snake appears to be associated with abnormal development of the eyes, so in-bred leucistic lines have definite problems. It seems likely that leucistic Corn Snakes eventually will be bred and become available.

This discussion of course only touches the high points of Corn Snake color breeds. Much more work by dedicated breeders is necessary to standardize the breeds until they are on the same par as Dog breeds, for instance, and can be traced through pedigrees. New mutations continue to appear as more and more Corn Snakes are bred in captivity, some not especially attractive, some very desirable, but all potentially salable if properly selected or crossed with other breeds. Breeding Corn Snakes to produce pure lineages is a difficult and time-consuming business, and it never fails to amaze me that so many individuals of so many types are available at such reasonable prices. Every hobbyist owes a debt to the scientists, breeders, and dealers who have spent years helping you obtain that beautiful, perfect Corn Snake.

GREAT PLAINS RAT SNAKES

HISTORY

West of the Mississippi River, the Red Rat Snake is replaced by the closely related Great Plains Rat Snake, *Elaphe emoryi*. This common snake of farmlands, river bottoms, and oases in moderately dry prairies first was described by Baird and Girard in 1853 on the basis of a specimen from Crockett County, Texas. Because of various misunderstandings, for many years it was known under the name *E. laeta*, later shown to be based on a subadult American Rat Snake (*E. obsoleta*). Though this western snake long was considered a full species, in the early 1950's it was relegated to a subspecies of *E. guttata*. However, recent collections along the eastern edge of the range in Louisiana and Arkansas have shown only a slight tendency for the Great Plains Rat Snake to assume the characteristics of the Red Rat Snake. For this reason many herpetologists feel that it deserves the rank of a full species, an opinion followed here.

There can be little doubt that the Great Plains Rat or a form remarkably like it was the ancestor of the Red Rat. Probably some two million years ago the species occurred over much of the present southern and western United States and northern Mexico. With the various glacial advances and retreats plus related changes in the giant Mississippi River valley, an eastern segment of the species became cut off from the basic western form and evolved in isolation into the Red Rat Snake, *E. guttata*, by assuming a brighter reddish, orange, or mahogany coloration. There are few significant differences in scale counts and structure between the Great

First described by Baird and Girard in 1853, the Great Plains Rat Snake, *Elaphe emoryi*, replaces the Red Rat Snake west of the Mississippi River.

PHOTO BY ISABELLE FRANCAIS.

Plains Rat and the Red Rat, and both forms show gradual changes of various types in the scalation over their ranges. A few Red Rat Snakes, especially from the southern Appalachians and some western Florida populations, are markedly browner than red coastal specimens and thus resemble the Great Plains Rat Snake, but such variation seems to be sporadic and not an expression of continuing gene exchange with the western species. The Great Plains Rat itself shows significant distinctions in color pattern and scalation over its range, so the eastern and western species appear to be continuing their evolution in different directions.

DESCRIPTION

In structure the Great Plains Rat Snake is virtually identical to the Red Rat Snake. The dorsal scale rows are in 25-27-19 rows in most specimens, with a tendency toward 25-29-21 the further south the species goes (as over much of Texas). There are 8 supralabial scales in almost every specimen and usually 12 to 14 infralabials (rarely 11). Of all the scale counts, only the infralabials are any help in separating *E. emoryi* from *E. guttata*, with almost all *E. guttata* having 11. Ventral scale counts vary greatly, from as few as 203 to 215 in the northwestern part of the range to 230 or more in Texas. (There is remarkably little detailed information available on the species in Mexico.) Subcaudal scales vary in much the same way, from as few as 63 in the northwest to as many as 78 in the south. The scales are nearly smooth, with the middle one to

The Great Plains Rat Snake displays great variation in both pattern and scalation over its range. Because of this, scientists have named a number of subspecies over the years, none of which currently are recognized as valid.

PHOTO BY ISABELLE FRANCAIS.

PHOTO BY JOHN IVERSON.

As far as things like scale counts are concerned, there really is very little difference between the Great Plains Rat and the Red Rat. However, now that the two snakes are separate, their evolutionary paths seem to be moving in different directions.

eight scale rows keeled; juveniles may entirely lack obvious keels.

The coloration is far from striking, consisting of olive-brown squarish saddles or blotches on an ashy gray ground color. The saddles have narrow but distinct blackish brown borders that are more prominent in adults than in babies. The middle of the back has a series of large saddles that often are narrow at the four corners and from 2 to 5 (rarely 6 or 7) scale rows long (narrow in the northwest, wider in the south). The saddles continue over the tail. Like many other characters, the saddle number varies from the northwest to the southeast, specimens from the northwest having many (often 45 to 50) narrower saddles over the back before the vent, the saddles fewer (29 to 40 or so) and wider in the south. A second row of small round spots alternates with the main dorsal row low on the sides, and often there are faint, irregular spots at the edges of the body.

Though the shades of brown and gray vary (juveniles being paler and somewhat brighter than adults) a bit, there is never more than a faint pinkish tinge present low on the sides; reds and oranges are absent. The pattern on the head and neck is like that of the Red Rat Snake, the most anterior blotch sending forward two arms that meet in a spearpoint between the eyes. A broad stripe runs over the snout, through the eyes, and back beyond the angles of the jaws to the lower neck. Like the rest of the body pattern, the head stripes are brown, edged with black. The belly is white with faint pinkish tinges at the rear of the scales and is covered with squarish black spots that often show a bluish iridescence. The spots often are paired on each ventral scale and, as in the Red Rat Snake, under the tail fuse into regular narrow black lines.

VARIATION

Few color variations have been reported in wild-caught specimens of the Great Plains Rat Snake, though albinos are known. There are repeated reports of weakly striped specimens in the literature, but I've yet to see a photo or good description of one. Occasional specimens from southern Texas have the dorsal saddles split down the middle and may represent a step toward a striped pattern.

As you can see if you bothered reading through the description above, there is a lot of variation in this species and it is related to geography. Once a subspecies was recognized, *E. emoryi intermontanus* Woodbury and Woodbury, described in 1942 to accommodate very odd specimens from an isolated group of populations in central eastern Utah and adjacent Colorado. This isolate was defined as having an average of 69 blotches on the body plus tail, each blotch only 2 to 4 scale rows long, in combination with averages of 209 ventral scales and 67 subcaudal scales (276 total). This would contrast

On the head of this particularly light specimen of *Elaphe emoryi* you can clearly see the characteristic "spearpoint" marking, the tip of which is on the frontal scale (on the top of the head).

PHOTO BY R.D. BARTLETT.

PHOTO BY ISABELLE FRANCAIS.

Although most Great Plains Rat Snakes boast the "spearpoint" marking on the head, sometimes this marking will be broken up, as it is on this specimen. This goes to show you the value of learning as many characteristics about an animal as possible. Don't rely on just one to make a reliable identification!

to more typical (i.e., Texas) specimens of *E. emoryi emoryi* with fewer blotches (average 50) on the body plus tail, each blotch 3 to 5 or 6 scale rows long; this form averages a total of 295 plates under the body, 223 ventrals and 73 subcaudals. Snakes from the northwestern populations also tend to be smaller than typical Great Plains Rats and often are so dark that it is difficult to count the number of blotches on the back.

Unfortunately, these counts appear to vary in a complex geographic pattern, and many specimens from Kansas and extreme western Texas, for instance, are intermediate in all respects. The subspecies *intermontanus* thus has been synonymized with *emoryi*, though it still has its supporters and, at least in the isolated Utah—Colorado populations, may be recognizable by easily seen color and pattern characters.

While this book was being written, Dr. Hobart M. Smith and three of his colleagues reevaluated variation in the Great Plains Rat Snake and came to an interpretation

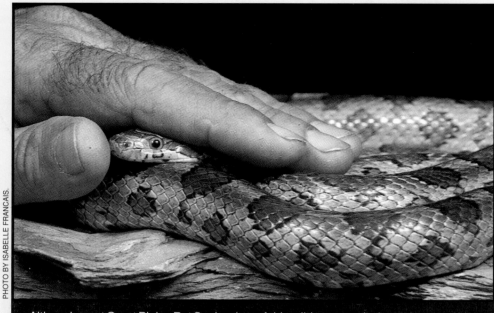

PHOTO BY ISABELLE FRANCAIS.

Although most Great Plains Rat Snakes have fairly mild tempers, it always is a good idea (as a safety precaution) to place your hand over their heads before grasping them.

different from that usually reached. They decided that variation in the snake is not clinal, but instead represents two distinct subspecies, one with low dorsal saddle counts (44.5 or fewer on the body) and the other with higher counts (45 and up). The low-count form is found in Arkansas, eastern Texas, and all the range of the snake in Mexico; it has been named *meahllmorum*. The high-count form is found over most of Kansas, Oklahoma, and New Mexico, plus central and western Texas, as well as the Utah—Colorado populations. Dr. Smith and company still consider the Great Plains Rat to be a subspecies of the Corn Snake, believing that the difference in color is insufficient for specific rank and that the Louisiana specimens really do represent intergrades. I have no idea how this new work will be received, but I find several problems with it and see no reason at the moment to either consider *emoryi* a subspecies of *guttata* or recognize the southern *meahllmorum* and northern *emoryi* as distinct subspecies, instead considering the Great Plains Rat Snake to not have subspecies (unless *intermontanus* is proved valid).

LENGTH

Like the Red Rat Snake, the Great Plains Rat is a rather small snake, average adults being 2 to 3.5 feet long, with a few specimens exceeding 4 feet. The record specimen seems to be one measuring in at a fraction of an inch over 5 feet.

Males seem to be a bit shorter than females and have a slightly longer tail, as in Red Rats.

RANGE

Great Plains Rat Snakes are common from the southern half of Missouri and most of Kansas south through virtually all of Texas. They become more uncommon and sporadic at the western edge of the range in eastern New Mexico and southeastern Colorado, and just enter Nebraska at the far north. At the northeastern edge of the range the species manages to cross the Mississippi River, ranging into Illinois for a few miles. To the south it extends well into Mexico to southern Coahuila and San Luis Potosi. The Mexican range is not completely known, and there are indications that the species is absent from much of the drier portions of the country. In fact, even in the western United States this snake may be restricted to moist riverbanks and oases, being unable to subsist in extremely dry areas. As mentioned, there is an isolated population in eastern central Utah and adjacent Colorado that must represent a relict of a much wetter Great Plains during one of the interglacial periods. Remember that the western United States presently is much drier than it was just a few thousand years ago, and the present distribution of the snakes and other herps represents disappearances of species from areas that have only recently become too dry to support the species.

Elaphe emoryi is uncommon in the dry, rolling pine hills of central Louisiana, eastern Texas, and southern Arkansas, and it once was thought that specimens from this area represented intergrades with the

This Great Plains Rat Snake came from a population in Kansas. *Elaphe emoryi* occurs over a good portion of the central and western United States and also into Mexico.

PHOTO BY JOHN IVERSON.

Red Rat Snake. Over the years, collecting effort has reduced the gap between these eastern localities and the major body of the species in Texas, and it seems likely that the species really is fairly widely distributed over all of Texas into central Louisiana and adjacent

NATURAL HISTORY

For such a wide-ranging and often common snake, this species is not especially well-known. Perhaps this is because it is nocturnal most of the year and thus not often seen except by collectors. That this is not a species of deep woods is fairly

PHOTO BY ISABELLE FRANCAIS.

The Great Plains Rat is a creature of open areas such as the edges of rivers and streams, farmlands, various prairielands, canyons, and caves. It is nocturnal throughout most of the year.

Arkansas. If this is true, *E. emoryi* is separated from *E. guttata* by the broad band of silty soils and swampy land that forms the western bank of the Mississippi River. In color and counts (including infralabial scales), central Louisiana specimens agree with more western *E. emoryi*, and leading Louisiana herpetologists feel that there is no intergradation between the two related and similar species in that state.

certain, most specimens coming from more open areas such as river and stream edges, sparse cottonwood areas near farmlands, prairies of various types, and canyons and caves in drier areas. It spends much of the day under cover such as rocks and logs or in rodent burrows. Though a good climber (the body is bread-loaf-shaped as in other American rat snakes), it usually is seen on the ground in active search of prey or mates.

The food consists of small rodents and other mammals (such as bats in the case of snakes inhabiting caves) and nestling birds killed by constriction. The young have been reported to eat treefrogs and lizards, but this probably is not essential prey and just a matter of eating what is available.

Man is the major predator today, though in the past coyotes, raccoons, birds of prey, and other snakes were the major enemies. The species is a good ratter and often is welcomed on farms, but it seems that some idiots never get the hint: it often is killed by those who somehow mistake it for a rattlesnake (like most *Elaphe*, it vibrates the tail when cornered and makes a rattler-like noise). I vividly remember seeing one such dead and battered specimen on display, strung over a barbed wire fence along a highway in New Mexico just west of El Paso—some people never learn or want to learn. Cars undoubtedly take a heavy toll at night, but fortunately much of the range of the species is sparsely settled and has few paved roads beyond a few major highways. The species is always available commercially as wild-caught specimens, so there is a fair amount of human "take," mostly in Oklahoma and New Mexico, I am told. Captive-bred babies also appear on the market with some regularity.

Great Plains Rat Snakes emerge from hibernation (brumation, if you wish) between the end of March and the end of April, and they disappear in September or October, depending on the severity of the winter in the local area. They have been found hibernating in communal hibernacula along with other species on several occasions. Mating behavior is much as described for the Corn Snake, also lacking a mating bite by the male on the female's neck. Copulation typically lasts the usual 15 to 30 minutes. Eggs in nature are laid in June and July and number anywhere from four or five to 20 or 30. The eggs are large, usually larger than those of the Red Rat Snake, typically from 2 to 2.6 inches long on the day laid. Like those of *E. guttata*, they vary from elongate to broadly oval in shape and may or may not have crystalline projections from the creamy white shells.

The young are hatched after a relatively moist incubation of 70 to 80 days (very approximate), usually being seen in September. At hatching they vary from nearly 10 to over 14 inches in length. When seen in the open, most young are at least 14 inches long. They may grow rapidly in nature, with one record of an increase from 9.5 inches to 29 inches in less than 14 months.

A one-eyed captive lived for 21 years and 2 months in a variety of zoos after it was captured as a full (though small) adult probably three years old. Expect captives to live at least a dozen years if given proper care.

CAPTIVE CARE AND BREEDING
Except for its somewhat shorter period of activity and

thus virtual lack of a second clutch, keeping and breeding the Great Plains Rat Snake is much like care and breeding of the Red Rat Snake and Corn Snake. Relatively few herpetoculturists maintain large colonies of the species because there is a very limited market— its coloration simply does not compare to that of even a dull Corn Snake or the brownest Red Rat. It seems that they are just as adaptable as Red Rats, however, and feed and grow at similar rates.

Given a choice, it seems that a male Great Plains Rat Snake will not mate with a Red Rat or Corn Snake. This has limited the actual number of crosses between the species in captivity, though once mating occurs it appears that the embryos

develop normally. The species has not yet shown a great tendency to mutate in captivity, but perhaps this is just because not enough litters have as yet been bred.

For most hobbyists their major interest in *Elaphe emoryi* is as a parent in producing "creamsicle" Corns. This pale orange breed is actually a hybrid of a normal Great Plains Rat Snake crossed to an albino Corn Snake. Remember that the Great Plains Rat naturally lacks significant orange pigments. The result is an amelanistic albino with pale orange saddles on a whitish ground with an orange tinge. As usual, such albinos are quite variable within a litter. The cross is genetically similar to that of albinism in the Corn Snake, a normal (*AA*) *E. emoryi*

Although Great Plains Rats have not set the herpetocultural world on fire, their genes seem to have been mixed in with some captive-bred Corn Snake varieties. This snake, for example, seems to have at least some Great Plains Rat in it (although exactly how much is unknown).

PHOTO BY PATRICK H. BRIGGS, COURTESY LLOYD LEMKE.

PHOTO BY W. P. MARA.

Shown is a neonatal example of the beautiful "creamsicle" Corn Snake, a product of an albino Corn crossed with a normal Great Plains Rat.

being crossed with an albino (*aa*) Corn Snake. Their offspring are externally (phenotypically) colored as normal for *E. emoryi* but of course are mixed or heterozygous (*Aa*) for albinism. When these offspring are mated to each other, they produce (theoretically) one-quarter albinos (creamsicles, in this case), half heteros or carriers for albino, and a quarter "normals." Since these are hybrids, however, do not expect either normal ratios of offspring nor uniformity of patterns at any step of the cross.

One difficulty with this cross is that, as mentioned, the species do not cross readily. The trick is to let a pair of either species begin the usual mating rituals and, just before actual copulation, quickly remove the female and substitute a breeding-ready female of the other species. In many cases the male will continue his mating behavior unless the female becomes especially aggressive. Large females and small males seem to work best. Be sure the same-species female is removed from sight and scent of the male or you won't have any luck. A similar procedure, equally fraught with uncertainty, is used to hybridize Corn Snakes with various other rat snakes, kingsnakes, milk snakes, and gopher snakes. If you produce **any** hybrids, please do not sell them as other than what they really are, or you could ruin someone's breeding program.

OTHER T.F.H. BOOKS BY THE AUTHOR

These and hundreds of other colorful and informative pet-keeping books are available from T.F.H. Publications. Check your local pet shop for more titles.